<u>One'</u> Sketches for the Solo Puppeteer

Written by Debbie Vincent

One To One Sketches For The Solo Puppeteer
Edited by Harry Barrett

ISBN 1-904172-06-7

A One Way UK Publication
First Published in Great Britain AD 2005
By One Way UK

One Way UK Creative Ministries
Unit 6 Robert Cort Ind Estate
Britten Road
Reading
RG2 0AU

Tel: 01189 756 303
Fax: 01189 313 008

E-mail: info@onewayuk.com
Web Site: www.onewayuk.com

Copyright ©2005 One Way UK Creative Ministries

All rights reserved. No part of this publication may be reproduced, stored in a retrieval system, or transmitted, in any form or by any means, electronic, mechanical, photocopying, recording or otherwise, without the permission, in writing, of the publisher. Permission is granted to the purchaser of this publication to make whatever copies of scripts are necessary for your personal use in your own church/school ministry.

One to One
Contents

Introduction

So where do I start?

	Scripture link
Sketch 1: It's Time for School	John 3 v 17
Sketch 2: Nursery Rhymes	Psalm 145 v 13b
Sketch 3: My Father's Eyes	Genesis 1 v 27
Sketch 4: A Touch of Retail Therapy	Hebrews 9 v 28
Sketch 5: My Gift is Me	Matthew 10 v 8b
Sketch 6: Life's Little Irritations	Hebrews 11 v 8
Sketch 7: I Will Always Love You	1 Chronicles 16 v 34
Sketch 8: Box Yourself In	Matthew 5 v 3
Sketch 9: Zap Me God	2 Chronicles 7 v 14
Sketch 10: Pretending Helps	Romans 15 v 7

Introduction

Solo puppetry and ventriloquism are one of the most dynamic and creative mediums for presenting the Christian message. They capture the minds and hearts of the audience with their light hearted and amusing appeal which does not obscure the depth of the message being delivered. They are fun to perform, easy to adapt to a variety of situations and stimulate the imagination.

A well rehearsed and thoughtfully presented sketch or story will appeal to all ages and hold the fascination of the audience. Come on then, let's go!

SO WHERE DO I START?

Here are eight helpful hints to keep in mind.

1. <u>Learn and know</u> the sketch off-by-heart, both your own and your puppet's parts. This is so that the sketch flows smoothly and naturally, maintaining its rhythm.
2. <u>Timing</u> will add dimension and impact to your presentation by slowing down or speeding up different sections to create an effect. Sometimes even silence can be powerful as either yourself or your puppet uses facial expressions and body language to keep the sketch ALIVE.
3. Your <u>relationship</u> with your puppet is crucial – you will need to know your puppet like a best friend, his/her habits, good and not so good characteristics. Their personality will need to be developed and brought out. Try not to make your puppet mirror your own character, he/she will need its own identity.
4. Don't be afraid to show <u>emotions</u>. Sympathise, empathise, laugh spontaneously in realistic situations with your puppet. Enjoy what you are doing and saying too, so that your audience can join in and share in the fun.
5. Remember to involve your audience in different ways. Eye contact is crucial between:
   a. Yourself and your audience
   b. Yourself and your puppet
   c. Your puppet and your audience.

   Your eyes and those of your puppet should be roughly the same height so be aware of where and how you are holding or positioning your puppet. Ensure that your audience, however large or small can easily see both of you. In the sketches, sometimes you directly mention one person in the audience, make sure you choose somebody you know who won't mind or you have prepared beforehand, you wouldn't want anyone to feel intimidated.
6. <u>The scripts</u> themselves are like a framework or skeleton. The can be used as they are printed on the page or you can adapt and modify them to fit yourself, your puppet and your own situation. Feel free to experiment with them, elaborate and emphasise the parts you want to, because ultimately you need to have ownership of your own presentation.
7. Sometimes a song is used to complement the sketch or bring it to a close. If you are able to sing it with your puppet it would be so effective or alternatively sing along with the recording or play the recording itself. You may prefer to choose your own song but remember, the words of the song need to be appropriate to the message you are presenting.
8. <u>Have a go</u>! Try your presentation out on friends and family. Let them help you improve it, but most importantly, I pray that God will bless your presentation as you are providing an opportunity for others to come to know more about His amazing love for us – Debbie.

SKETCH 1

IT'S TIME FOR SCHOOL

We can all find reasons to avoid doing things especially those that have become a matter of routine. In this sketch the puppet make obvious excuses that we have all probably used especially in our school days. As the sketch develops, the puppet realises for him/herself that he/she has not been truthful and there is a situation that he/she is trying to avoid. Eventually, through the dialogue, the puppet acknowledges the need to be honest with God and him/herself, to accept His forgiveness not only for the action or thought itself, but also for the avoidance of its consequences.

God did not send His Son, Jesus, to condemn and remind us of our failures, but rather to forgive us and save us from the guilt of our own shortcomings.

Scripture link

John 3:17 'For God did not send his Son into the world to condemn the world, but to save the world through him' (NIV)

IT'S TIME FOR SCHOOL

[*Curtain opens with Puppeteer & puppet dressed in pyjamas*]

Puppeteer	(*Name of Puppet*), you're in your pyjamas?
Puppet	Yes that's right, it's Saturday, I'm having a day off.
Puppeteer	But it's Tuesday, you've got school today, you need to be dressed.
Puppet	That's not fair.
Puppeteer	Sorry, why?
Puppet	Someone has stolen the weekend and I didn't notice.
Puppeteer	(*Puppet name*), it's Tuesday. You have to go to school, just like all the other children here.
Puppet	But I'm not like the other kids you know, I'm a purple reject (*or colour of puppet*).
Puppeteer	It's the law (*puppet name*), you have to go to school unless you're not well enough.
Puppet	(*squeaks*) I've just remembered I've got a sore throat.
Puppeteer	Well (*Puppet name*) you were fine last night singing in the shower.
Puppet	It happened in the night, yes that's it, I've lost my voice.
Puppeteer	You have not lost your voice (*Puppet name*), you were speaking to me just a minute ago, remember?
Puppet	It's your conscience speaking!
Puppeteer	Look at the time, you must get dressed.
Puppet	It's no good, I can't go.
Puppeteer	You haven't got a temperature, you're not hot?

Puppet	I may not feel hot but just look at me? I look hot don't I, look at my colour!
Puppeteer	That's your normal colour (*Puppet name*), you're absolutely fine. Now come on!
Puppet	No, no I can't go to school today (*Puppet shakes her head*)
Puppeteer	But (*Puppet name*), you must go to school, there is nothing wrong with you, you'll be fine as soon as you get there.
Puppet	No, I'm not allowed.
Puppeteer	You're being silly now, of course you're allowed.
Puppet	I'm not, I've got … you know.
Puppeteer	I don't know, tell me?
Puppet	I can't, it's rude, you told me not to say bad words.
Puppeteer	Then whisper it to me.
Puppet	Are you sure?
Puppeteer	Yes I am very sure [*speaks firmly to Puppet*]
Puppet	Oh (*Puppet whispers*)
Puppeteer	I can't hear you (*Puppet name*), say it again, a bit louder this time.
Puppet	Nits
Puppeteer	Sorry
Puppet	NITS
Puppeteer	Nits
Puppet	Yes NITS NITS NITS 'N' 'I' 'T' 'S' [*says each letter individually*]
Puppeteer	You haven't got nits (*Puppet name*), I washed and combed your hair last night, I didn't see any nits.
Puppet	They're microscopic nits, special puppet breed, you need a puppet scope to see them you know.

Puppeteer	Well, ok, now what's the problem, why don't you want to go to school?
Puppet	Aaaachoo!
Puppeteer	You haven't got a cold (*Puppet name*), everyone sneezes now and again. (*Puppet name*), just tell me the truth, what's happened?
Puppet	(*Puppet hesitates, then reluctantly replies*) I've got a heart ache (*Puppeteer name*) [*leaning on Puppeteer*]
Puppeteer	A heart ache? I've heard of a stomach ache but what's a heart ache?
Puppet	It's a pain right here (*points to heart*)
Puppeteer	When did it start?
Puppet	Yesterday, in maths.
Puppeteer	In maths, what happened?
Puppet	A piece of rubber hit my teacher on the back of her head while she was writing on the board.
Puppeteer	Well how did that give you a heart ache?
Puppet	Tom said it was my fault and he said he saw me throw the rubber.
Puppeteer	Well that wasn't very nice, (*Puppet name*), but you didn't throw the rubber did you?
Puppet	W .. e .. l .. l .. (*spoken very loudly with a guilty tone and expression*)
Puppeteer	(*Puppet name*) you didn't did you?
Puppet	Well it was a good shot though wasn't it?
Puppeteer	(*Puppet name*)!
Puppet	Well I didn't mean to, I was bored and it sort of pinged off the end of my ruler.
Puppeteer	You should not have done that (*Puppet name*), but it's no good running away from it. It's good to own up, admit that you did

9

	something wrong, say sorry, and ask Jesus to forgive you, (*Puppet name*) you will feel much better inside.
Puppet	Are you sure?
Puppeteer	Yes (*Puppet name*).
Puppet	Are you sure you're sure?
Puppeteer	(*Puppet name*) don't start that again. I'm certain, you will feel a lot happier and that smile will be back on your face. The smile that God wants to see because he has forgiven you and loves you. (*Puppet slowly turns his/ her solemn look into a smile*)
SONG	I've got a smile on my face. (Great Big God 2)

SKETCH 2

NURSERY RHYMES

I'm sure, like me, you sometimes feel you've put your foot in it and said completely the wrong thing at the wrong time, even to the wrong person! Yes, and I know that I have made promises that I have not been able to keep. It is so easy to feel let down by other people and forget about the times we have let down others ourselves, even those who are very close to us. Nursery rhymes is a very light hearted sketch where the puppeteer and puppet become quite 'picky' with each other. Both characters agree in the end that God never lets us down, He is always there for us because His promises never fail.

Scripture Link

Psalm 145 v 13b 'The Lord is faithful to all His promises and loving towards all he has made' (NIV)

NURSERY RHYMES

[Puppet is pulling Puppeteer onto the stage very noticeably]

Puppet	I wish you'd put a bit more effort into your entry (*Puppeteer name*). You're a bit of a slow coach. I want to be centre stage. I want to be a star!
Puppeteer	I'm doing my best (*Puppet name*), performing is not just about what happens on stage, there are things to be done behind the scenes too.
Puppet	Like what may I ask?
Puppeteer	Like checking the final arrangements with the stage manager and ...
Puppet	Oh Harold you mean or Harry should I say, we are on familiar terms you know! (*referring to and turning head to look at Harry Barratt or other person familiar to your audience eg minister/elder etc*).
Puppeteer	(*Puppet name*), behave yourself. I think maybe we need to work on your attitude a little. (*Puppet gasps in horror*) Performing is about working as part of a team. We need to rely on each other and try to understand each other and (*Puppet interrupts*)
Puppet	Even when we get things wrong, like coming on to stage late (*Puppeteer name*)!
Puppeteer	Yes ok, but we need to support each other. (*Puppet looks around her body*)
Puppet	Support did you say, support? Where am I sagging? It can't be my fault if my posture isn't right can it? (*glares directly at Puppeteer*)
Puppeteer	I'm just saying (*Puppet name*) that we need to work as a team ... together.
Puppet	Are words important too? (*snuggling head into Puppeteer's shoulder*)
Puppeteer	Of course they are, (*looking at Puppet fondly*) otherwise we wouldn't know what is happening next and speaking of words it's about time we started on your nursery rhyme recital.
Puppet	(*Puppet repositions herself*) Ok then here goes. Checklist first – number 1 – posture (*looks about him/herself*); number 2 – lights

	(*looks up to lights which could flash on and off in acknowledgment*); number 3 – sound ... I said SOUND (*shouts*) [*Puppeteer covers his/her eyes with despair and embarrassment*]
Puppeteer	And don't forget ...
Puppet	Me! [*Puppeteer shakes head*] You! (*shakes head and looks at ground*) Harry! [*Puppeteer puts hand over Puppet's lips*]
Puppeteer	Us, a team remember. But I was thinking of diction (*Puppet name*), diction.
Puppet	(*head sways from side to side as if mimicking*) diction, diction, diction.
Puppeteer	(*Puppet name*), nursery rhyme recital now, please.
Puppet	(*adjusts herself again*) diction, see I haven't forgotten! [*Puppeteer is now completely exasperated by his/her 'friend' Puppeteer looks around as if he/she wants nothing at all to do with Puppet*]
	[sing nursery rhymes to original tunes]
Puppet	Humpty Dumpty sat on a wall Eating a big ice cream, He dropped a bit down Mary's back And she began to scream (*Puppet screams*)
Puppeteer	(*Puppet name*), those aren't the words we were taught.
Puppet	Oh well, shall I try another one then? Here goes – Baa Baa black sheep Have you any cash No sir, no sir Just lots of trash
Puppeteer	(*Puppet name*), I think you are just doing this on purpose! Before we came onto stage you promised me that you would do your very best and now look what you're doing.
Puppet	I can't see a problem, I'm singing with my best voice.
Puppeteer	But with the wrong words!

Puppet		The audience don't seem to mind, (*Puppet sighs and snuggles head onto Puppeteer's shoulder*) Give me one more chance please? I'll say the right words.
Puppeteer		Ok (*Puppet name*), but this really is your last chance.
Puppet		Ok, best till last (*Puppet repositions herself*)

Twinkle twinkle chocolate bar,
How I wonder where you are
In the fridge or on the side?
When I find you we will hide
Twinkle, twinkle chocolate bar,
Tummy wonders where you are (*look at tummy*)

Puppeteer		(*Puppet name*), you promised me, in front of everybody here
Puppet		(*Puppet surveys audience*) Even that man there with the curly hair?
Puppeteer		(*Puppet name*), when you promise to do something it means you are going to try your hardest to do what you said you would.
Puppet		(*thinking and scratches head*) I know I haven't kept my promise (*Puppeteer name*), but I do know someone who never lets us down. God is always there for us. He'll even help us when we get the words wrong.
Puppeteer		You're right (*Puppet name*). He is ready to help us in every part of our lives.
Puppet		Even when we get things wrong. Hey (*Puppeteer name*) shall I sing another nursery rhyme!
Puppeteer		No, three is enough for one day. And besides, I think the stage manager is waiting to talk with us.
Puppet		Harry (*or other person familiar to audience*), - I'd forgotten about him. I hope he won't be too upset with us.
Puppeteer		With you, you mean.
Puppet		I don't know what you are talking about – and besides, didn't you say we should be working as a team?
Puppeteer		(*sighs and shakes head as they leave the stage*)

SKETCH 3

MY FATHER'S EYES

Our eyes seem to give away so many secrets about ourselves. They can even express how we are feeling; especially about ourselves. One of the most incredible things I find about being a Christian, is that God accepts me as I am and loves me for who I am. With this in mind, I hope that when other people look at me, they will not only see me as a person, but will also have a glimpse at our Father, for He is our Creator.

Scripture Link

Genesis 1 v 27 So God created people in his own image; God patterned them after himself; male and female He created them. (NIV)

SKETCH 3

MY FATHER'S EYES

(*Puppet tries to get comfortable on his/her seat, Puppeteer helps him/her to settle and gently places his/her hand under Puppet's chin*)

Puppeteer	Now, (*Puppet name*) promise me you will be good on stage. Just this once please!
Puppet	Oh all right then I'll try.
Puppeteer	Good! Now are you comfortable? [*looking Puppet up and down*]
Puppet	I could do with a velvet cushion (*Puppet looks at the hard stand on which he/she is sitting*)
Puppeteer	But (*Puppet name*) only royalty get velvet cushions!
Puppet	Well I'm royalty at heart you know! (*looks at Puppeteer indignantly*)
Puppeteer	(*Puppet name*) come on stop this now, or what will everyone think? (Puppet name) please this is a very pre ... prestu .... Pre ..
Puppet	Prestigious! Humph.
Puppeteer	Thank you, what he/she said, place.
Puppet	(*sniffing and sobbing sounds*)
Puppeteer	Now (*Puppet name*) what's wrong? Come on stop crying and tell me what's the matter.
Puppet	(*Puppet sniffs*)
Puppeteer	(*Puppet name*), don't do that, look use a tissue.
Puppet	But I don't have one.
Puppeteer	Here use mine (*holds out a tissue for Puppet*)
Puppet	Are you sure you haven't used it?

Puppeteer	Yes! I'm sure.
Puppet	Are you sure you're sure?
Puppeteer	Yes I'm sure I'm sure. Now, blow your nose please [*Puppeteer passes Puppet a tissue*]
Puppet	Honk honk.
Puppeteer	(*Puppeteer name*) what are you doing?
Puppet	I'm blowing my nose, honk honk.
Puppeteer	All right that's enough (*Puppet name*).
Puppet	Can I look at the bogies?
Puppeteer	No you cannot! Now tell me what's wrong.
Puppet	I never had one.
Puppeteer	Had what?
Puppet	You know in the dressing room.
Puppeteer	Well I had everything that I needed in the dressing room. I mean, make-up, clothes, mirror. Oh (*Puppet name*) did you see the mirrors that had all the light bulbs going around the edge! [*head moves in a circular motion*]
Puppet	That just goes to prove it! I never had one; I never had a mirror with all the light bulbs going round the edge (*head moves in a circular motion to imitate Puppeteer*). I obviously take second place!
Puppeteer	(*Puppet name*) you know that's not true.
Puppet	I'm a reject, a purple reject (*dependent on colour of puppet*)(*tosses head back*)
Puppeteer	(*Puppet name*) you know that's not true either!
Puppet	You didn't come here in a suitcase!
Puppeteer	Well I know that, but we came in the same car.
Puppet	But I was in the boot! (*Puppet spits on the floor*)

Puppeteer	Oh! (*Puppet name*) don't do that, it's disgusting.
Puppet	Even worse than looking at bogies?
Puppeteer	Yes, even worse!
Puppet	Wicked! (*big smile on face and looking directly at audience*)
Puppeteer	(*Puppet name*) …..
Puppet	I'm a QS, quality second.
Puppeteer	Oh no here we go again!
Puppet	No wait, I'm a UFO.
Puppeteer	A UFO? (*Puppet name*) you know you can't fly.
Puppet	Uncared for Fabric Object silly.
Puppeteer	(*Puppet name*), you know how important I am … I … I mean how important you are.
Puppet	See! That just goes to prove it.
Puppeteer	(*Puppet name*) you know how important you are.
Puppet	You mean you know how important you are (*Puppeteer name*), and besides, look, look at my nose.
Puppeteer	But there's nothing wrong with your nose. Is there? There's nothing wrong with it is there? [*directed at audience*]
Puppet	It's stitched onto the end of my face, mind you look at the size of his honker (*look at one person in the audience*)
Puppeteer	(*Puppet name*) stop it now, don't be so rude!
Puppet	He's been telling a lot of lies.
Puppeteer	Lies! What do you mean by lies?
Puppet	Just like Pinnochio!
Puppeteer	(*Puppet name*) stop it!
Puppet	He doesn't have to take a suitcase on holiday with him does he?

Puppeteer	(*Puppet name*)!
Puppet	It's easy, he packs his trunk!
Puppeteer	(*Puppet name*) no! I don't believe you are doing this!
Puppet	I bet if he went round a corner too fast he'd poke someone's eye out with that thing.
Puppeteer	[*Puppeteer laughs*] (*Puppet name*) stop it.
Puppet	You've got a really funny laugh (*Puppeteer name*).
Puppeteer	Well at least I don't laugh like a donkey.
Puppet	No I don't (*but laughs like a donkey*)
Puppeteer	Look (*Puppet name*) what's brought all this on?
Puppet	I'm different.
Puppeteer	Well how'd you mean you're different?
Puppet	Sometimes I don't know who I am, I don't know who (*Puppet name*) is (*Puppeteer name*)!
Puppeteer	Oh (*Puppet name*) Aaah. [*encourages audience to sympathise by gesturing with hand*) So that's what this is all about. Look (*Puppet name*) it doesn't matter how different we are we have to be happy with ourselves just the way we are. And of course that's the way God loves us, just the way we are!
Puppet	Aah, I see ….. (*but shakes head*0 No, I'm sorry I don't understand.
Puppeteer	Well (*Puppet name*), come look very closely into my eyes and tell me what you can see. (*Puppet puts his/her nose very close to Puppeteer and peers intently into his/her eyes*)
Puppet	I can see a …. I can see an eye ball!
Puppeteer	Yes (*Puppet name*), but look closely, look very closely. What can you see?
Puppet	(*excitedly*) an eyelash ooh and something black. Are you sure you haven't got a fly in there? Hold on a minute, yes I can see your … your … (*Puppeteer name*) you've got your Father's eyes!

Puppeteer	That's right (*Puppet name*), let me explain what it means to have my father's eyes.
SONG	My Father's Eyes (One Way Street 'Top Solo Songs')
Puppet	Now I understand, but I still think a velvet cushion might have helped!

SKETCH 4

A TOUCH OF RETAIL THERAPY

In our busy, hectic world it is so easy to be distracted especially by bargains! There are so many tempting offers – buy 1 get 1 free (if you can find them), buy 1 get 1 half price, 3 for the price of 2 and so on. But only one person paid the ultimate price, our saviour and our friend Jesus. There were no conditions to the sale, no 'ifs' only unconditional love. How often do we need a '2 minute silence' to remember the price He paid for each of us.

Scripture Link

Hebrews 9 v 28 'So Christ was sacrificed once to take away the sins of many people, and he will appear a second time, not to bear sin, but to bring salvation to those who are waiting for him. (NIV)

SKETCH 4

A TOUCH OF RETAIL THERAPY

(Puppet and Puppeteer walk onto stage chatting together)

Puppeteer	Here we are again (*Puppet name*), Saturday evening, hey and didn't we have a good time today?
Puppet	Well some of us might have (*rather grumpily*)
Puppeteer	Oh come on! It wasn't that bad and I remember [*pauses*] yes (*Puppet name*) that place! Maybe we won't be going there again, it was a bit difficult wasn't it?
Puppet	Difficult – listen to you – I have never been so utterly embarrassed. I don't know how people can call it therapy.
Puppeteer	Therapy, how do you mean?
Puppet	Oh come on you know, everyone's going on about it, you know – good old retail therapy.
Puppeteer	Oh shopping!
Puppet	It was supposed to be one of your better ideas.
Puppeteer	But you were the one who wanted to spend some of Dad's money (*or another person of your choice*).
Puppet	Excuse me! It was my first experience of shopping in Blue Water [*name local shopping centre*].
Puppeteer	Yeah, right – I thought it would be nice, you know, a good day out – a treat.
Puppet	Treat did you say? Treat! Well, I left myself in your capable hands and look what happened. I mean you told me to get in the car and belt-up I mean to say, I wasn't even talking!
Puppeteer	I was talking about your seat belt (*Puppet name*), not you.
Puppet	So you say, I'm going to tell all these lovely people what I have to put up with.
Puppeteer	What you have to put up with? That's unbelievable (*Puppet name*)!

Puppet	Ok, I'll tell everyone then. You told me we were going to the park and for a ride, and where did we end up? At a car park with a bus stop!
Puppeteer	I explained it to you (*Puppet name*), we were going to park the car out of town and ride on the bus to the shopping centre. I wish you would listen – it helps to ease the congestion in town.
Puppet	For whom might I ask, the bus was so packed I was the one who was congested, I was chokerphobic.
Puppeteer	I think you mean, you felt claustrophobic
Puppet	No I was chokerphobic by the smell of that man's feet opposite me. And to make it worse the bus didn't stop at the shop I wanted.
Puppeteer	That's because it goes to the centre for everybody.
Puppet	And when we did get there I couldn't get on the moving stairs, they wouldn't wait for me to jump on.
Puppeteer	(*Puppet name*) it was an escalator, it takes people up to the next floor, besides you didn't have to stop it.
Puppet	But IT did say push the red button in an emergency … and I did.
Puppeteer	I know, it was so embarrassing, everybody thought it was me.
Puppet	Yes I know! (*Puppet laughs*)
Puppeteer	Oh (*Puppet name*) what am I going to do with you?
Puppet	And I didn't like the shops anyway, all those signs saying 'try me' most of it was disgusting, tasted nothing like blueberries.
Puppeteer	That's because it was cream for your complexion, you rub it into your skin to make you feel soft and silky, most people don't eat it.
Puppet	I don't need cream, all I need is fabric softener. And then! That shop assistant was so rude, asking me if I would like a free facial, there's nothing wrong with my face! And to top it all that man wouldn't let me take a free sample.
Puppeteer	No (*Puppet name*) the one you took was not free. The Security Guard thought you were trying to shop lift.

Puppet	I told him not to be stupid, do I look as if I can lift a shop?
Puppeteer	(*Puppet name*), he was trying to explain that you can't walk out of the shop without paying first.
Puppet	So, I was running out of time, I needed to go somewhere.
Puppeteer	Well, you could have asked to be excused for a minute and you didn't need to keep jumping up and down!
Puppet	But you didn't understand, I needed to go urgently, desperately in fact, my bowels were bursting!
Puppeteer	You only had to say you needed the toilet.
Puppet	Oh no I didn't.
Puppeteer	(*Puppet name*) you did, you should have said you needed to visit the toilet urgently, immediately in fact.
Puppet	That was only the start of my problems, then the lady waiting at the door asked me for 10 pence.
Puppeteer	Well that's ok (*Puppet name*), she has to take care of the area and make sure it stays clean and hygienic.
Puppet	Ok that might be the case, but I would only like to have paid 5 pence for that paper. I mean, a person in my position needs double quilted, super soft. Just think what might have happened if I'd have got a paper cut – ouch!
Puppeteer	The trouble was (*Puppet name*), we spent so long doing everything else, I only had time to buy one T-shirt.
Puppet	And what did I end up with, nothing! Absolutely nothing fitted me at all. There were only 8, 10, 12's what about those of us that are 11?
Puppeteer	(*Puppet name*), those were sizes not ages, there was a special section for small people like yourself.
Puppet	Special section indeed, petit, what's petit? [*spoken as pet – it*]
Puppeteer	Petite (*Puppet name*), petite!
Puppet	It's spelt pet-it.

Puppeteer	But it's pronounced petite (*Puppet name*), it's French.
Puppet	OOOh cava j'ai (*Puppet name*) j'ai belle.
Puppeteer	Stop it (*Puppet name*).
Puppet	Why?
Puppeteer	I don't know anymore French!
Puppet	But I am multicultural you know, I can do German too, Guten Tag, Auf Widensein.
Puppeteer	(*Puppet name*)!
Puppet	Switzerland (*yodelling*)
Puppeteer	(*Puppet name*) stop it.
Puppet	Oh mama mia!
Puppeteer	(*Puppet name*) we are in England.
Puppet	Howdy partner!
Puppeteer	(*Puppet name*) behave! You're really annoying me!
Puppet	Je t'aime, I love you. (*rests head on Puppeteer's shoulder*)
Puppeteer	Oh what am I going to do with you!
Puppet	No what am I going to do with you (*Puppeteer name*) – and just remember, who paid for your top!
Puppeteer	Oh I'm sorry I forgot about that. I'll give you the money back so you can pay my dad back.
Puppet	I DO charge interest you know.
Puppeteer	(*Puppet name*)!
Puppet	It was worth a try. Just think about it, what are friends for?
Puppeteer	Lots of things (*Puppet name*), like listening to each other, being there for each other, having ….
Puppet	Jesus as our friend.

Puppeteer	Well remembered (*Puppet name*).
Puppet	An didn't he do some buying.
Puppeteer	Well, he certainly paid for things.
Puppet	Yeah, like us, Jesus paid the full price for us by dying in our place.
Puppeteer	You're right and there's something more. Jesus is all we need.
Puppet	I would still like my money back (*Puppeteer name*).

SKETCH 5

MY GIFT IS ME

This sketch can not only fit brilliantly into any service around Christmas time but at other times too because we all like receiving presents and gifts. On the other hand, it's just as pleasurable to give gifts to other people and share the joy of giving and receiving together. In 'My gift is me, the puppet completely misses the point, seeing giving as a way of impressing. Isn't it a privilege and honour to offer our gifts and talents to Our Father who so freely gave to us.

Scripture Link

Matthew 10 v 8b 'Freely you have received, freely give.' (NIV)

SKETCH 5

MY GIFT IS ME

Parcel Force (pronounced par – cel in a French accent) a starch and rigid square character.

Parcel	Oh my, I really don't know if this is where I should be. I mean, look at all of these people, they're not the sort of people I'm accustomed to acquainting with.
Puppeteer	That's not a very nice way to introduce yourself is it?
Parcel	Yes, of course it is, one has to establish just who one is you know. My father for a start, is a Duke.
Puppeteer	Oh that's very interesting! He's the Duke of where? What's his name?
Parcel	He is the Duke Box of the Rovers Return in Coronation Street.
Puppeteer	That is a grand title.
Parcel	Oh and don't forget my mother, she works at the palace, Buckingham Palace you know.
Puppeteer	Wow! Has she met the Queen? What does she do at the palace?
Parcel	No dear, she's not exactly in the palace as such. She is in employment outside of the Queen's bedroom in fact.
Puppeteer	Oh!
Parcel	Yes, she is the Royal Flower Box you know. Now before we get too far (*puppeteer's name*), I need your help. I'm trying to think of some ideas for my brother's birthday present.
Puppeteer	That should be quite easy, what sort of things does he like?
Parcel	It's not so much what he likes my sweet, it's more what I like. After all, one would go nowhere else than Harrods. I'd have to buy him the biggest, newest, most expensive present that I could find.
Puppeteer	Don't you think that he would prefer something that he would like?

Parcel	My love, I don't know who brought you up but one must always impress others.
Puppeteer	I don't agree, my brother likes his play station and so, I would probably buy him a new play station game, if it's not too expensive!
Parcel	Oh the poor boy, how very sad! Now the trouble with my brother is that he is always getting fed up and bored.
Puppeteer	Why's that, he must like to do something?
Parcel	Well, he's a cardboard box you see, [*play on pun – bored/board*], he is rather a problem to us, he has no style, no glamour like the rest of us.
Puppeteer	Money doesn't mean everything you know.
Parcel	It does if you are a money box my child.
Puppeteer	No, that's not what I mean, you shouldn't give someone a present just because it's best for you, yourself.
Parcel	How extraordinary! If you don't spend a lot of money, your gift means nothing at all. Surely you must realise that little fact.
Puppeteer	No it's not how much you spend, it's how much you give.
Parcel	Excuse me my dear, look at me, look at just how much I could give.
Puppeteer	How can I explain this, the best gift any of us could ever give costs no money at all.
Parcel	How dreadful!
Puppeteer	No, how wonderful, God gave his only son Jesus so we would know how to live.
Parcel	Oh yes, I think I've heard that somewhere … on a Sunday in church probably, and as we are speaking of such matters you should see me on a Sunday when I go to church, my golden papers glisten in the morning sun. And of course everyone can hear my gold coins clatter as they fall into the collection plate. God must be so pleased with me.
Puppeteer	Well my gift to God is not like yours at all.
Parcel	Oh my pet, how terrible.
Puppeteer	No, the greatest gift I can give is … is … me, yes me, you see my gift is me!

Parcel	Well that's certainly different to say the least, can't you explain it more clearly to me?
Puppeteer	I know I can, listen to my song.
Song	My Gift is Me.

SKETCH 6

LIFE'S LITTLE IRRITATIONS

From the day we are conceived, we are changing, developing, growing in many different ways, physically; emotionally; mentally; spiritually. It is always such a comfort to know that God knows us far better than we know ourselves. We have all been through those situations when a very small incident becomes a greater irritation which can grow quite out of proportion. How do we cope? Where do we turn to for help? Who will guide us? How do we stay 'in control'? Yes, you know too, by looking to Jesus Himself, who doesn't change, who is ultimately dependable, thank you Lord!

Scripture Link

Hebrews 13 v 8 Jesus Christ is the same yesterday, today and forever. (NIV)

SKETCH 6

LIFE'S LITTLE IRRITATIONS

[Par-cel Force is a domineering, almost patronising, rather old fashioned school ma'am]

Parcel   Now come along, come along dear folks, settle down, settle down now. That's it, now let's begin with our register:

Curtis E Car	
Ellie Kopter	*(slight pause between each, where*
Anna Rack	*puppeteer groans sympathetically*
Arthur Ritus	*along with audience)*
Oliver Sudden	
Sam Widge	
Urika Garlic	
Tish U, *(pause)* hello, I said tissue.	

Puppeteer   I don't think she's here miss, I can't see her anywhere.

Parcel   No, no, I mean, I need a tissue for myself, now dear *(patronising tone)* where was I ... oh yes ...my dear child *(puppet looks at member of audience)*, straighten that tie, brush your hair out of your eyes and pay attention – all of you! *(glancing around at audience)*. Now focus your thoughts, the One Way School is very selective you know, we don't accept anybody. Now as I was ... [*knock from a door interrupts puppet*]

Puppeteer   Miss Force, excuse me, there's somebody at the door.

Parcel   Then see who it is my child.

Puppeteer   Yes of course Miss Force. *(puppeteer looks towards door)* There's somebody to see you Miss, I think they would like the register.

Parcel   Then pass it to him, as quickly as you can, this is really spoiling this morning's lesson. *(Puppeteer pretends to pass register)* Yes, P ... S ... H ... E ... personal, social and health education, this is all about how one takes care of oneself. For this you need to ... *(louder knocking on a nearby door)*.

Puppeteer   Miss Force, I'm afraid there's someone to see you again.

Parcel   Ignore it, just ignore it and I'm sure they'll go away. *(Even louder knocking interrupts)*

Puppeteer	They're still waiting Miss Force.
Parcel	Just leave them I say, they'll soon go aw ... *(louder knocking and puppet clears throat)*. Hum, hum, yes you need to look after yourself in lots of ways ... If something starts to <u>irritate</u> you (*emphasise 'irritate'*) you need to find a way to stay calm and ... (*knocking is loud and rigorous*).
Puppeteer	They're not going away Miss Force.
Parcel	Calm and (*said quietly*) ... Quiet! (*loudly*). Yes, my children, you've got to learn to block out life's little irritations from your mind. Breathe in *(pause and encourage audience to join in with you)*, ... breathe out. Let's all do that together (*knock, knock*) AGAIN!
Puppeteer	Miss Force, they're not going away, I think they want the dinner register this time.
Parcel	Then, let them take it, let them take it, NOW! Now, returning to my lesson – no matter what happens, self control is the answer to all of life's <u>little</u> annoyances. There are several techniques that can ... (*very loud knocking*).
Puppeteer	You forgot to give them the dinner money this time Miss Force.
Parcel	That can (*in a high, tense voice*) help with <u>any</u> of life's annoyances. Counting to ten helps you remain cool and avoid ... (*exceptionally loud knocking!*)
Puppeteer	What would you like me to do Miss Force?
Parcel	Let me just look at my class and remind myself – young man, stop picking your nose (*directed at someone in the audience who can accept this remark*) and ... Adam and Eve over there, I don't care what the snake said, just put that apple down! As I was saying, no matter how you are feeling just ... (*repeated knocking, puppet opens mouth and shakes head as if screaming but no sound*)
Puppeteer	God is always there for you isn't he Miss Force? (*Puppet is awe-struck and looks around at audience with mouth left open*)
Parcel	What did you say my child?
Puppeteer	Well Miss Force, you see, no matter how <u>we</u> (*emphasised*) are feeling, God, Our Father, well, He doesn't change. Miss ... He is always there for us, no matter how we are feeling.

Parcel   You mean, God can even help us with life's little irritations? (repeated/loud knocking)

Puppeteer   Yes Miss, especially with life's little irritations!

SKETCH 7

I WILL ALWAYS LOVE YOU

Sometimes we can really feel excited and get prepared for an event that can turn out completely differently to our original expectations. Our interpretations can all be so varied. This can sometimes be due to our own misunderstanding. There is however, only one interpretation from God's word, the Bible, which is resoundingly strong and clear – God says to each of us, 'I will always love you.'

Scripture Link

1 Chronicles 16 v 34 Give thanks to the Lord, for he is good! His faithful love endures forever. (NIV)

SKETCH 7

I WILL ALWAYS LOVE YOU

[*Parcel is admiring herself*]

Parcel   Yes, yes, I think that will do nicely. One must take care of oneself my dear child. Oh, oh what a nuisance there's a blot on one of my eyelashes. Do be a dear and help me, I must look my absolute best. (*Puppeteer peers into Parcel's eye and takes away the unwanted eyelashes*)

Puppeteer   Better? But Parcel, what is all the fuss about, why have you got to look your best today?

Parcel   Oh my goodness! Don't you know? ... But look at what you are wearing, do run along and get changed, that outfit won't possibly do!

Puppeteer   What do you mean Parcel, it's my best dress/suit.

Parcel   Oxfam must have been very busy the last time you were in town.

Puppeteer   Parcel, I feel really offended – my mum bought it for me.

Parcel   Well that just explains it then.

Puppeteer   Parcel, don't be so rude.

Parcel   If it wasn't me, someone had to say it. Oh look my dear, today I am expecting a ... VIP no less.

Puppeteer   A VIP? A very important person you mean?

Parcel   That is a possibility, but no my dear a VIP in this instance is a <u>very</u> (*emphasised*) important present.

Puppeteer   How do you know it will be arriving today and isn't it a bit unusual to dress up for a ... a ... package?

Parcel	Darling, never underestimate any situation in life.
Puppeteer	Come on Parcel, there's got to be something you're not telling me.
Parcel	Well, I suppose you've got to know sometime my sweet love (*Parcel coughs*). I have been contacted by a secret admirer, in a very high place.
Puppeteer	Wow Parcel, who is it, come on tell me.
Parcel	Ooh I don't quite know how to explain this, I have received a message from a Royal Male. (*emphasise the pun male/mail*)
Puppeteer	Aah, well, that's great but where is the message, let me see it. What does it say?
Parcel	Now, don't run before you can walk my dear child! I haven't received it as yet.
Puppeteer	I don't understand, you're expecting a very important present from a royal male and you haven't got the message yet?
Parcel	Well, when I returned home yesterday, I had a postcard delivered by a delightfully smart smiling man, oh, I do like men in uniforms.
Puppeteer	Well go on … what did it say?
Parcel	It said, or rather <u>he</u> said 'He would be coming to call upon me this evening to present one with a VIP'.
Puppeteer	So this is why you got yourself ready.
Parcel	I am certain the rolls will be arriving any moment my child.
Puppeteer	But I'm not hungry, I've eaten.

Parcel	We need to do something about your education my dear, I was referring to the Rolls Royce motor car. One would expect nothing less from a person of Royal status.
Puppeteer	Hey Parcel, I can see the postman coming.
Parcel	He's obviously one of my regular visitors my dear.
Puppeteer	Do you think you might have got it wrong, scrambled the message or something?
Parcel	How could you suggest such a thing my mind is perfect, I think?
Puppeteer	Parcel, here comes your Royal 'Male'. (*smug laugh*)
Parcel	Don't be silly, that's just the . . . .the . . I can't quite see, that eyelash is back in my eye again.
Puppeteer	Parcel, look – the postman has brought you this letter and he <u>works</u> for the <u>Royal Mail</u>.
Parcel	So are you implying the person who delivered this letter is employed by a Royal Male.
Puppeteer	No Parcel, the Royal Mail, they deliver letters, parcels, boxes, lots of things all over the country. Shall we open it?
Parcel	Well, I'm not quite so certain now, it looks as though I've got myself ready for, ready for … nothing really. I don't think I've ever received a very important message in my life before.
Puppeteer	You have Parcel, it's the most incredible message that has been sent for all of us.
Parcel	For me as well you mean? You'd better tell me more.

Puppeteer	God has given us His message in the Bible, (*point to Bible*) it is the message about His love for us.
Parcel	And this, this message, do I need to dress up for it?
Puppeteer	Hardly Parcel, but you can if you want to.
Parcel	What's the main point of it again?
Puppeteer	God says in His message, Parcel, 'I will always love you'.

You might like to finish the sketch with either a performance or recording of the song His love Goes On (Righteous Pop Music 4).

SKETCH 8

BOX YOURSELF IN

In the Beatitudes, Jesus teaches us about the amazing hope and freedom he has brought to us. Yet, so often we shut ourselves in and restrict ourselves. In this simple sketch, the puppet spends much of the time talking from inside of a box. We see that we don't need to 'box' ourselves in because God can see all the wonderful things we can do in His strength and not our own – He seeks only to bless us.

Scripture Link

Matthew 5 v 3 God blesses those who realise their need for him, for the Kingdom of Heaven is given to them. (NIV)

Sketches 8, 9 and were originally written to be used with 'Henry Bear'. Some direct references are made to a bear but these can easily be adapted to suit your own puppet.

SKETCH 8

BOX YOURSELF IN

Puppeteer	(*talking directly to audience*) Before we start I just want to tell you that I'm not here because I'm the best ventriloquist; I'm just the best in the price range. Hey (*puppet name*) cheer up, I thought that you were going to give me some help tonight?
Puppet	I can't.
Puppeteer	Why not?
Puppet	I'm not worthy oh spotless one.
Puppeteer	What do you mean?
Puppet	Well, I could tell them about the big spot on the end of your nose if you want me to.
Puppeteer	Ha! Why would you want to do that?!
Puppet	He/she's got one on his/her … (*puppeteer places hand on puppet's mouth to muffle sound*)
Puppeteer	Stop it.
Puppet	… And one on his/her cheek.
Puppeteer	(*Puppet name*)!
Puppet	(*laughs & whimpers*) Oh, you're right, I'm a mean old bear. No one should love me! I … what is that? (*looking at a large empty cardboard box*)
Puppeteer	Well, obviously it's a cardboard box.
Puppet	You're supposed to be comforting me!
Puppeteer	Sorry.
Puppet	I'm ashamed of myself, I should go and live in something like that. (*puppet goes into the box*) Hello (hello, hello), (*echo gets quieter as puppet peeps into the box*). Is (is is), any (any any), one (one one), there (there, there)? (*Looking back at Puppeteer*) Hey! It's a big box you know, I'm just going to have a look inside.

Puppeteer	(*Puppet name*) this isn't going to help you.
Puppet	Good, I don't deserve any help.
Puppeteer	Why? What have you done?
Puppet	I'm mean, mean, mean! I'm a mean old thing.
Puppeteer	What could you have done that's so horrible?
Puppet	When I was at cubs, I bit one of the other *bear's* ears and now none of them like me.
Puppeteer	(*Puppet name*) you didn't!
Puppet	No, I mean I didn't do anything.
Puppeteer	Hold on, you did, you just said so. You just said you bit one of the other puppet's (*bear's*) ears!
Puppet	I didn't!
Puppeteer	You did!
Puppet	I didn't!
Puppeteer	(*puppet name*) You did!
Puppet	Fine, I did!
Puppeteer	Oh you didn't!
Puppet	What do you want me to say?!
Puppeteer	Well, I must admit that wasn't very nice, but why would you want to bite his ear in the first place?
Puppet	I was hungry. I need my protein! Wait … who am I kidding, no one could love me. I'm going to hide myself in that box. (Puppet is lowered into box so that only its voice can be heard.)
Puppeteer	(*Puppet name*) God loves you and he doesn't care what you've done in the past because he can see the future and all of the good things that you could do.
Puppet	God's not real.
Puppeteer	Yes he is, He's just as real as you and me.

Puppet	But I can't see him.
Puppeteer	You can't see anything, you're in a box.
Puppet	Picky!
Puppeteer	(*Puppet name*) I can't see you at the moment but it doesn't mean that you're not real, we shouldn't 'box' ourselves in with the bad things that we've done. We can still hear and feel God. Now, I don't care whether you are in that box or not, I'm going to sing a song.
Puppet	I don't want to sing.
Puppeteer	Why not?
Puppet	(*Puppet leaps up from inside box*) I'm going to rap.
Puppeteer	That sounds like fun, let's hear it then!

Rap: God is really, really Real
    (Real Kids Worship, Mark Thompson)

SKETCH 9

ZAP ME GOD

There are so many technological advances at the moment with 'instant' responses to commands. It's so easy to click a switch, push a button or even enter a PIN number. These have so many advantages in an age where communication has a place of priority. Yet, it is simply incredible that we have always had a direct line with God through prayer, a line that doesn't run out of credit or need to be 'topped up'.

Scripture Link

1 Chronicles 7 v 14 If my people who are called by my name, will humble themselves and pray and seek my face ... then I will hear from heaven ... (NIV)

SKETCH 9

ZAP ME GOD

Puppet	Hey, hey (*puppet name*) what do you think of this one then? (*Puppet looks in direction of a mobile phone – this could be a real one/cardboard or inflatable one*)
Puppeteer	It's not bad I suppose but …
Puppet	So, so what about this one? (*Crazy Frog ring tone plays – pre-recorded – or latest ring tone in fashion. Puppet jogs up and down in time to the music*)
Puppeteer	Oh please no!
Puppet	It's great isn't it? But I mean what kind of a frog is he? He's only wearing a hat and jacket. (*This will need to be updated depending on ring tone selected*)
Puppeteer	(*Puppet name*) you're only wearing a hat and a jacket.
Puppet	Yeah, but I've got style. Get with the time. The future is bright, the future is (*Puppet name*)!
Puppeteer	Whatever you say (*Puppet name*) but there was nothing wrong with your old ring tone, what do you need a new one for?
Puppet	(*Puppeteer name*) you have gone down in my estimation. Cool it babe, new phone, new ring tone to go with it.
Puppeteer	But (*Puppet name*) 'babe', this is your 3rd new phone this year, what's the point in replacing them all the time?
Puppet	I can't believe you have just asked me that question. You've got to keep up with the fashion, everyone knows that.
Puppeteer	Well, where did you get it from anyway?
Puppet	E pay, where else?
Puppeteer	E pay, don't you mean ebay?
Puppet	No, like I said 'e pay, my dad, well 'e pay for me every time and look – this is the latest model, it's even got a camera. You in the front row – smile – (*pause while puppet looks at mobile phone*) – here he looks better this way up!

Puppeteer	(*Puppet name*) that's so superficial.
Puppet	I'm not superficial, I just don't like ugly people.
Puppeteer	(*Puppet name*) you need to be sensible.
Puppet	(*Puppet name*) Hey listen, I've got a caller, just listen to that tune, (*chosen ring tone is played*). Hello, hello, yeah Mum, British Airways £59, no I'm at a puppet thingy, funny people, oh all right, I'll see you later (*Puppet mimics voice from BA advert*). That was my mum (*looking at audience*)
Puppeteer	We all heard.
Puppet	Well, I'm going to text my friend.
Puppeteer	How are you going to do that, you're sort of lacking in the thumbs department.
Puppet	There are other ways (*Puppet name*) babe, watch this. (*Puppet bangs phone with his nose*)
Puppeteer	Ouch, doesn't that hurt you?
Puppet	Not me, I have padding in the right places. But I'll tell you the truth.
Puppeteer	Go on then.
Puppet	I bought the latest model so that I can have a direct line with God, the big man himself, I can call him in a flash and he can zap me back.
Puppeteer	Who told you that you could phone God?
Puppet	The nice salesman.
Puppeteer	Oh really, well – you don't need the latest phone to do that, you can talk to God anytime, anywhere through prayer.
Puppet	No!
Puppeteer	It's always been that way and it doesn't cost anything.
Puppet	Well, I'm going to try it anyway. (*Pre-recorded ring tone is played and puppeteer speaks the phone part, if venting is not possible this could be pre-recorded also*)

Phone	Thank you for calling God direct. All of our operators are busy at the moment. Your call is in a queue and will be answered as soon as possible.
Puppet	This can't be right, this is the latest model. (*looking cautiously at the mobile phone*)
Puppeteer	Sssssh! I think you're through.
Phone	Thank you for holding, please select one of the following options: Press 1 to leave an adorational prayer Press 2 for a confessional prayer Press 3 if you are praying for yourself Press 4 if you are praying on someone's behalf Press 5 to talk to one of the apostles.
Puppeteer	I think I might do that.
Phone	Please select one of the following options by pressing the hash key. Press 1 to talk to Peter Press 2 to talk to Paul.
Puppet	I'm thinking, Peter.
Phone	I'm sorry but Peter is not available at the moment, he is on gate duty. Please leave a message after the tone … (*beep*). I'm sorry I did not hear that correctly, please leave a message after the tone … (*beep*). I'm sorry, I did not hear that correctly.
Puppet	So much for latest gadgets.
Puppeteer	Don't worry (*Puppet name*), remember what I said, you can talk to God anytime, anywhere.
Puppet	And there's no call charge?
Puppeteer	None at all, all calls to God are free!
Puppet	Wow, cool or what, zap me Lord!.
Song	Zap me Lord God (Myles Bing)

SKETCH 10

PRETENDING HELPS

When I was younger, everyone I met seemed to ask me the same question, ' … and what would you like to be when you grow up?' Of course my answers varied at different ages and stages in my life. But I'm so glad now that I don't have to make something up or pretend to be something I'm not. I am completely, utterly and totally accepted; what a privilege and responsibility then, to accept other people around me.

Scripture Link

Romans 15 v 7 So accept each other just as Christ has accepted you; then God will be glorified (NIV)

SKETCH 10

PRETENDING HELPS

(*Puppet and Puppeteer walk onto stage whilst the puppeteer introduces them*)

Puppeteer	Hello everyone I'm (*Puppeteer's name*) and this is my friend (*Puppet name*). We're here to tell you about something truly incredible (*puppet is gazing around not paying attention*) Aren't we (*puppets name*)
Puppet	(*Instead of replying, puppet starts meowing, making cat noises*)
Puppeteer	Erm … what are you doing?
Puppet	I'm pretending, I'm pretending to be a … a cat!
Puppeteer	And you make a lovely cat but …
Puppet	(*Instead of replying, puppet starts barking, making dog noises*)
Puppeteer	Now what are you doing?
Puppet	I'm pretending to be a … a dog! (*barks again to emphasis the point*)
Puppeteer	Yes that's very nice but …
Puppet	(*Instead of replying, puppet starts mooing, making cow noises*)
Puppeteer	Oh let me guess, you're pretending to be a cow?
Puppet	Yep, how did you guess! (*rather sarcastically*)
Puppeteer	I don't understand, why are you making all of these animal noises?
Puppet	Because it helps me.
Puppeteer	What do you mean it helps you?
Puppet	It's embarrassing, I'm not sure if I can tell you.
Puppeteer	Well it can't be that bad.
Puppet	Well alright then, I have a real problem, I can't roar. (*Roar has been chosen since the puppet used in this sketch is Henry bear, but it would be easy to substitute another sound, even that of a human, such as sneezing or coughing for example*)

Puppeteer	What do you mean you can't roar? You're a bear (*if appropriate*), go on, give it a go!
Puppet	Well, ok, I'll try - (*Using lots of breath to whisper*- Rooaarr!) See I can't roar, I can't do it.
Puppeteer	Well why don't we get everyone here to help us? Here's what we are going to do. After I've counted to three I want all of you to roar (*or other selected sound*) as loudly as you can. Are you ready? 1 … 2 … 3. (P*uppeteer encourages audience to join in after the count and attempt a roar or other sound as fitting*)
Puppet	(*Puppet tries to hide as if now afraid of audience*) They're scary!
Puppeteer	Oh come on, why don't you give it a go?
Puppet	Here goes then, I'll count myself in, after three, 1 … 2 … 3 (Puppet roars loudly) Oh thank you everyone!
Puppeteer	I knew you could do it!
Puppet	That's because I had a little help from my friends, didn't I? Hey, wait wait, can I make one more sound please?
Puppeteer	Oh go on then.
Puppet	Do you know what you are (*Puppeteer's name*)?
Puppeteer	Please tell me.
Puppet	Cuckoo! Cuckoo! (*sniggers as they leave the stage with puppeteer shaking head*